CompTIA IT Fundamentals FCO-U61 Practice Exam

(New Edition)

No Answers Spoiling

-Answers are found at the end of the book-

By EXAM BOOST

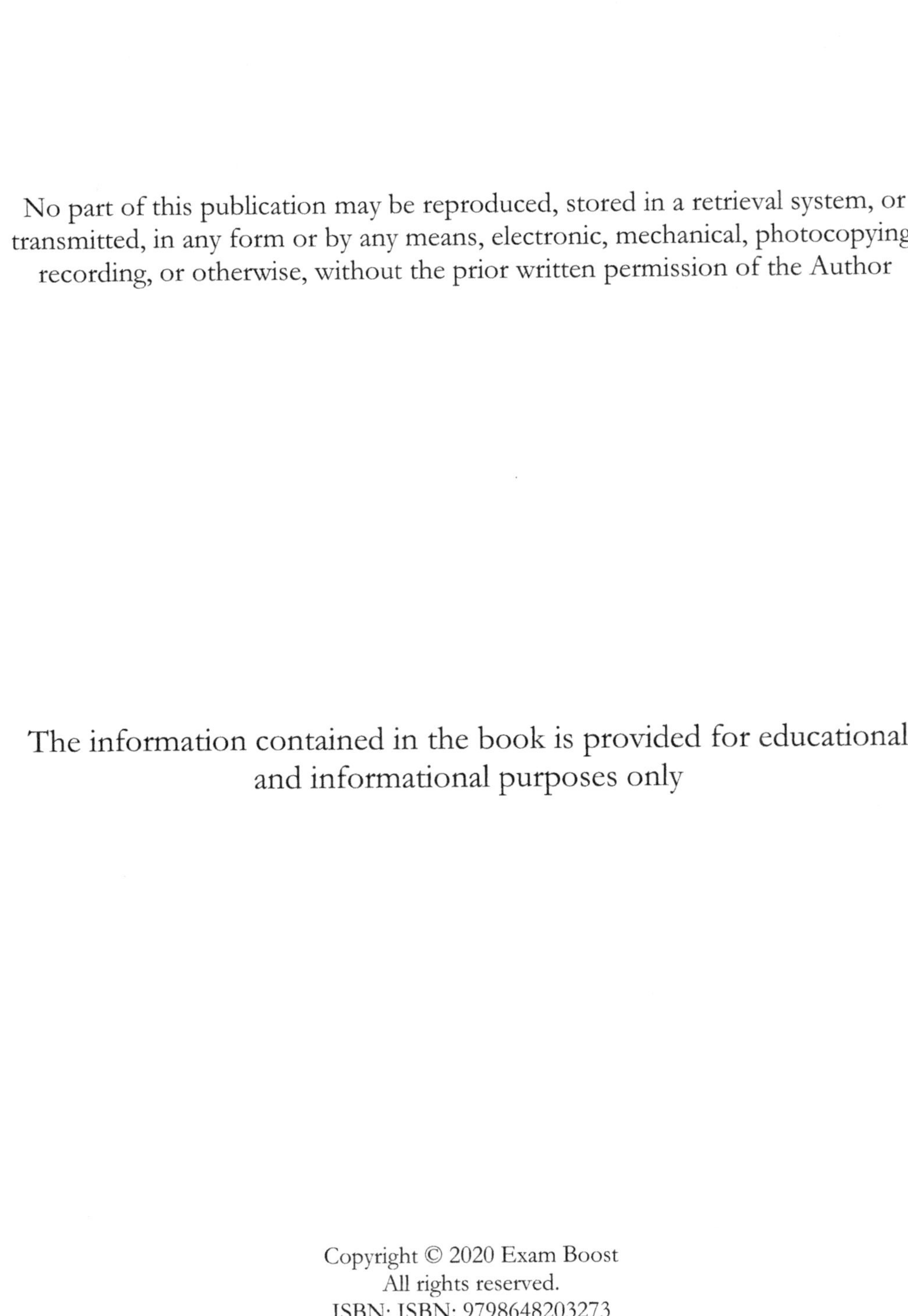

The information contained in the book is provided for educational and informational purposes only

ISBN: ISBN: 9798648203273

Pass IT Fundamentals FCO-U61 Exam in First Attempt Guaranteed.

This book contains Real Exam Questions, Accurate & Verified Answers as Seen in the Real Exam.

Vendor: CompTIA
Certifications: CompTIA IT Fundamentals
Exam Name: CompTIA IT Fundamentals
Exam Code: FCO-U61
Total Questions: +190 Questions and Answers

CompTIA ITF+ helps professionals to decide if a career in IT is right for them or to develop a broader understanding of IT.

- ITF+ is the only pre-career certification that helps students or career changers determine if they have a competency for information technology and if it is the right career path for them.
- ITF+ is the only single certification that covers all areas of IT foundations, creating a broader understanding of IT making it ideal for non-technical professionals.
- ITF+ establishes an IT education framework for students in middle school and high school.

EXAM 1

QUESTION 1
Which of the following allows wireless devices to communicate to a wired network?

A. Modem
B. Switch
C. Firewall
D. Access point

QUESTION 2
Which of the following computing devices would be used to provide a centralized means to distribute services to a group of clients and usually possesses a role on a LAN?

A. Laptop
B. Workstation
C. Mobile phone
D. Server

QUESTION 3
Which of the following BEST describes an application running on a typical operating system?

A. Process
B. Thread
C. Function
D. Task

QUESTION 4
The broadcast signal from a recently installed wireless access point is not as strong as expected. Which of the following actions would BEST improve the signal strength?

A. Update from 802.11b to 802.11g.
B. Ensure sources of EMI are removed.
C. Enable WPA2-Enterprise.
D. Use WiFi Protected Setup.

QUESTION 5
A systems administrator uses a program that interacts directly with hardware to manage storage, network, and virtual machines. This program is an example of:

A. a storage area network.
B. an embedded OS.

C. network attached storage.
D. a Type 1 hypervisor.

QUESTION 6
Which of the following is a compiled language?

A. Perl
B. JScript
C. Java
D. PowerShell

QUESTION 7
Which of the following actions is the FINAL step in the standard troubleshooting methodology?

A. Document the solution and cause.
B. Create a new theory of cause.
C. Research the problem online.
D. Implement preventive measures.

QUESTION 8
Which of the following is a value that uniquely identifies a database record?

A. Foreign key
B. Public key
C. Primary key
D. Private key

QUESTION 9
A systems administrator wants to return results for a time range within a database. Which of the following commands should the administrator use?

A. SELECT
B. INSERT
C. DELETE
D. UPDATE

QUESTION 10
Which of the following statements BEST describes binary?

A. A notational system used to represent an "on" or "off" state

B. A notational system used to represent media access control
C. A notational system used to represent Internet protocol addressing
D. A notational system used to represent a storage unit of measurement

QUESTION 11
A program needs to choose apples, oranges, or bananas based on an input. Which of the following programming constructs is BEST to use?

A. Variable
B. If
C. Datatype
D. Comment

QUESTION 12
A UPS provides protection against:

A. denial of service
B. replay attack.
C. power outages.
D. wiretapping.

QUESTION 13
A company executive wants to view company training videos from a DVD. Which of the following components would accomplish this task?

A. Optical drive
B. Hard disk drive
C. Solid state drive
D. Flash drive

QUESTION 14
A technician is troubleshooting a problem. The technician tests the theory and determines the theory is confirmed. Which of the following should be the technician's NEXT step?

A. Implement the solution.
B. Document lessons learned.
C. Establish a plan of action.
D. Verify full system functionality.

QUESTION 15
Given the following pseudocode:

```
program Breakfast
weekday = ["Monday", "Tuesday", "Wednesday", "Thursday", "Friday"]
weekend = ["Saturday", "Sunday"]
  if today == Wednesday
    output "Bacon and eggs"
  else if today == Firday
    output "Oatmeal"
  else if today in weekend
    output "Waffles"
  else
    output "Pancakes"
end
```

If the Breakfast program ran on Sunday, which of the following would be the output?

A. Oatmeal
B. Bacon and eggs
C. Waffles
D. Pancakes

QUESTION 16
Which of the following BEST describes a kilobyte?

A. A kilobyte is a measurement of storage (e.g., 100KB).
B. A kilobyte is a measurement of throughput (e.g.,100Kbps).
C. A kilobyte is a measurement of power (e.g., 100KW).
D. A kilobyte is a measurement of processor speed (e.g., 2.4KHz).

QUESTION 17
Which of the following security concerns is a threat to confidentiality?

A. Replay attack
B. Denial of service
C. Service outage
D. Dumpster diving

QUESTION 18
Which of the following software license models allows a developer to modify the original code and release its own version of the application?

A. Proprietary software

B. Commercial software
C. Open source software
D. Cross-platform software

QUESTION 19
Which of the following are the basic computing operations?

A. Input, process, output, and feedback
B. Input, output, storage, and feedback
C. Input, process, and output
D. Input, process, output, and storage

QUESTION 20
Which of the following is a wireless communication that requires devices to be within 6in of each other to transfer information?

A. Infrared
B. NFC
C. Bluetooth
D. WiFi

QUESTION 21
The IT department has established a new password policy for employees. Specifically, the policy reads:

- Passwords must not contain common dictionary words
- Passwords must contain at least one special character.
- Passwords must be different from the las six passwords used.
- Passwords must use at least one capital letter or number.

Which of the following practices are being employed? (Select TWO).

A. Password lockout
B. Password complexity
C. Password expiration
D. Passwords history
E. Password length
F. Password age

QUESTION 22
Which of the following would MOST likely prevent malware sent as compromised file via email from infecting a person's computer?

A. Email previewing
B. Patching
C. Clear browsing cache
D. Kill process

QUESTION 23
A user wants to use a laptop outside the house and still remain connected to the Internet. Which of the following would be the BEST choice to accomplish this task?

A. Thunderbolt cable
B. Bluetooth module
C. Infrared port
D. WLAN card

QUESTION 24
Joe, a user, finds out his password for a social media site has been compromised. Joe tells a friend that his email and banking accounts are probably also compromised. Which of the following has Joe MOST likely performed?

A. Password reuse
B. Snooping
C. Social engineering
D. Phishing

QUESTION 25
Which of the following network protocols will MOST likely be used when sending and receiving Internet email? (Select TWO.)

A. SMTP
B. POP3
C. SNMP
D. DHCP
E. ICMP
F. SFTP

QUESTION 26
A database administrator finds that a table is not needed in a relational database. Which of the following commands is used to completely remove the table and its data?

A. UPDATE
B. DELETE
C. ALTER

D. DROP

QUESTION 27
Ann, the president of a company, has requested assistance with choosing the appropriate Internet connectivity for her home. The home is in a remote location and has no connectivity to existing infrastructure. Which of the following Internet service types should MOST likely be used?

A. Fiber
B. DSL
C. Cable
D. Satellite

QUESTION 28
Which of the following language types would a web developer MOST likely use to create a website?

A. Interpreted
B. Query
C. Compiled
D. Assembly

QUESTION 29
A startup company has created a logo. The company wants to ensure no other entity can use the logo for any purpose. Which of the following should the company use to BEST protect the logo? (Select TWO).

A. Patent
B. Copyright
C. NDA
D. Trademark
E. EULA

QUESTION 30
Which of the following would be BEST to keep the data on a laptop safe if the laptop is lost or stolen?

A. Host-based firewall
B. Strong administrator password
C. Anti-malware software
D. Full disk encryption

QUESTION 31
Which of the following data types should a developer use when creating a variable to hold a postal code?

A. Integer
B. String
C. Float
D. Boolean

QUESTION 32
A function is BEST used for enabling programs to:

A. hold a list of numbers.
B. be divided into reusable components.
C. define needed constant values.
D. define variables to hold different values.

QUESTION 33
A game developer is purchasing a computing device to develop a game and recognizes the game engine software will require a device with high-end specifications that can be upgraded. Which of the following devices would be BEST for the developer to buy?

A. Laptop
B. Server
C. Game console
D. Workstation

EXAM 2:

QUESTION 1
Which of the following is a common characteristic of open source software?

A. Update cycles are dictated by the manufacturer
B. Modifications to core functionalities are made by the manufacturer
C. Can only run on certain manufacturer processors
D. Can be fully modified by the user

QUESTION 2
Which of the following operating systems is available for free and can be modified by anyone?

A. Windows
B. Linux
C. Mac OS
D. Chrome OS

QUESTION 3
Which of the following software package types is designed to accept input from multiple users?

A. Utility
B. Operating system
C. Specialized
D. Collaborative

QUESTION 4
A user learns of an operating system vulnerability that would allow a hacker to access the computer. The user would like to keep the operating system up to date to prevent such vulnerabilities from occurring. Which of the following should the user configure?

A. Additional OS features
B. Automatic updates
C. Software firewall
D. Anti-malware software

QUESTION 5
Which of the following is the BEST example of productivity software?

A. Word processing software
B. Entertainment software

C. Image editing software
D. Anti-malware software

QUESTION 6
A user has downloaded an application file with the .dmg file extension. Which of the following operating systems can be used with this file by default?

A. iOS
B. Windows
C. Mac OS
D. Chrome OS

QUESTION 7
By default, which of the following types of operating systems can automatically detect a user's location while the user is traveling in a bus?

A. Server
B. Desktop workstation
C. Virtual server
D. Mobile

QUESTION 8
A user had to replace the hard drive in a computer. The user would like to install the games that came with the computer but were not installed as part of the initial OS setup wizard. The user can install the games by performing which of the following?

A. Schedule automatic updates.
B. Enable installed OS features.
C. Update hardware drivers.
D. Reinstall productivity applications.

QUESTION 9
Which of the following features of a smartphone controls the screen orientation?

A. Gyroscope
B. NFC
C. Accelerometer
D. GPS

QUESTION 10
A user's operating system is set to automatically update as updates are released. However, last week's updates failed to download. Which of the following should the user

do FIRST to install the updates?

A. Reference the OS manufacturer's website.
B. Run a virus scan to remove viruses.
C. Reinstall the operating system.
D. Change the automatic update schedule.
E. Manually download the updates.

QUESTION 11
Which of the following printer types uses a powder based consumable with a lower cost per page compared to other printers?

A. Thermal
B. Laser
C. Dot matrix
D. Inkjet

QUESTION 12
A user installing a printer can connect it to which of the following ports? (Select FOUR).

A. PS/2
B. VGA
C. DVI
D. USB
E. FireWire
F. Serial
G. RJ-11
H. Parallel

QUESTION 13
When considering backup media, which of the following holds the MOST data?

A. BD-R
B. DVD-R
C. DVD-DL
D. CD-ROM

QUESTION 14
Which of the following printers requires a special type of paper in order to print?

A. Impact

B. Thermal
C. Inkjet
D. Laser

QUESTION 15
Which of the following components provides the FASTEST medium for hosting and storing an operating system?

A. Blu-Ray disc
B. 7200RPM HDD
C. SSD
D. DVD-RW

QUESTION 16
Which of the following computer components are used to store data? (Select TWO).

A. GPU
B. HDD
C. RAM
D. NIC
E. CPU

QUESTION 17
Which of the following connectors consists of three separate plugs for video?

A. Display port
B. S-video
C. Thunderbolt
D. Component

QUESTION 18
Which of the following allows for the FASTEST printer connections?

A. Bluetooth
B. USB
C. Parallel
D. Serial

QUESTION 19
Before purchasing a new video card for a PC, which of the following should be checked to ensure there will be enough electricity for the video card to function properly?

A. GPU
B. CPU
C. GUI
D. PSU

QUESTION 20
Which of the following has the lowest latency?

A. SSD
B. NAS
C. Blu-Ray
D. DVD

QUESTION 21
Which of the following is considered an optical storage medium?

A. SSD
B. Blu-Ray
C. Flash drive
D. Memory card

QUESTION 22
Which of the following are examples of keyboard connectors? (Select TWO).

A. USB
B. RJ-11
C. Serial
D. FireWire
E. PS/2

QUESTION 23
Which of the following is the function of a CPU?

A. Encrypts data for remote transmission
B. Performs data computation
C. Supplies electricity to components
D. Provides storage location for files

QUESTION 24
Several users want to share a common folder with high availability. Which of the following

devices is BEST to use for this requirement?

A. Large USB flash drive connected to a PC
B. Medium capacity SATA hard drive
C. Network attached storage appliance
D. Firewall with security management

QUESTION 25
Which of the following is a 15-pin video connection?

A. DVI
B. S-video
C. Component
D. HDMI
E. VGA

QUESTION 26
A laptop owner, Ann, can no longer see web pages when she opens her browser, and she can only see her search bars and plug-ins. Which of the following is the MOST likely source of this issue?

A. The computer does not have current antivirus software installed
B. The computer needs to have its components upgraded
C. The downloaded toolbars are filling the browser screen
D. The owner was not using complex passwords

QUESTION 27
Which of the following is the MOST sensitive Personally Identifiable Information (PII) and should be shared cautiously and only with trusted resources?

A. Email address
B. Phone number
C. Mother's maiden name
D. Last name

QUESTION 28
A user will be traveling with a smartphone that contains confidential information. Which of the following should be disabled? (Select TWO).

A. Keyboard
B. Speakers
C. Mouse

D. Bluetooth
E. NFC

QUESTION 29
A technician wants to minimize the risk of having third parties track previously visited web pages. Which of the following should be performed in the Internet browser's settings? (Select TWO).

A. Select form data
B. Disable location services
C. Remove cookies
D. Clear history
E. Change passwords

QUESTION 30
When setting up a new device, there are multiple features available that will never be used. Which of the following should the user do to make the new device more secure?

A. Make all users administrators.
B. Remove or disable the unnecessary features.
C. Install a password manager on the device.
D. Make all users guests.

QUESTION 31
Joe, a user, saves a document to a flash drive on his computer in order to print the document from a public computer kiosk. After returning home and reinserting the flash drive in his computer, the security software identifies an infected file on the flash drive. Which of the following is the MOST likely cause of the infection?

A. The flash drive was infected by a war driving hacker on the way to the public kiosk.
B. The public workstation was infected by Joe's flash drive.
C. The public workstation was infected and passed the virus to the flash drive.
D. The flash drive was already infected by the user's computer.

QUESTION 32
A user is browsing the Internet when suddenly a threatening message appears on screen demanding a payment in order to avoid the system being disabled. Which of the following BEST describes this type of malware infection?

A. Ransomware
B. Adware
C. Spyware

D. Virus

QUESTION 33
Which of the following is an example of ransomware?

A. A user is asked to pay a fee for a password to unlock access to their files.
B. A user receives an email demanding payment for a trial application that has stopped working.
C. A user has opened an Internet browser and is taken to a site that is not the normal home page.
D. A user is asked to open an attachment that verifies the price of an item that was not ordered.

QUESTION 34
An employee, Joe, forgot his laptop at the airport. Joe is worried about unauthorized access. Which of the following BEST protects against data theft in this instance?

A. Security software
B. Full disk encryption
C. Cable lock
D. Username and password
E. Patching the OS and third party software

QUESTION 35
Multiple laptops that contain confidential data are stolen from a company. Which of the following is a likely policy change resulting from this incident?

A. Enabling full disk encryption
B. Requiring screensaver password
C. Disabling Bluetooth adapters
D. Adding multifactor authentication

QUESTION 36
A user receives an email formatted to appear as if the bank sent it. The email explains that the user must confirm the name, address, and social security number listed on the bank account. Which of the following BEST describes the security threat taking place?

A. Shoulder surfing
B. Social engineering
C. Spam
D. Phishing

QUESTION 37
A user, Ann, is concerned about theft of her laptop and does not want a thief to have easy access to all of her banking and email. Which of the following precautions could be taken to mitigate this issue?

A. Only browse the Internet on WiFi connections that use WPA2
B. Turn off the guest account in the operating system
C. Disable autofill functionality within the web browser
D. Remove any legacy browsers from the computer

QUESTION 38
A user is configuring a new wireless router. Which of the following should be done to ensure that unauthorized changes cannot be made?

A. Change the SSID
B. Change the router's address
C. Change the administrator password
D. Change the encryption key

QUESTION 39
Which of the following would BEST be described as password best practices? (Select THREE).

A. Use of long passwords
B. Sharing passwords with a trusted source
C. Limiting password reuse
D. Keeping default passwords
E. Use of special characters
F. Writing down difficult passwords

QUESTION 40
A user, Ann, receives a call asking for her password to troubleshoot a problem. Which of the following describes this type of security threat?

A. Malware
B. Social engineering
C. Spam
D. Physical security

QUESTION 41
Malware that has an embedded keylogger to capture all of the keystrokes and steal logins is considered:

A. adware
B. spyware
C. ransomware
D. phishing

QUESTION 42
Which of the following security threats occurs when a user receives an email from an illegitimate source asking for login information?

A. Hacking
B. Phishing
C. Spam
D. Cracking

QUESTION 43
Which of the following are best practices when it comes to using a computer in a public location? (Select TWO).

A. Notify the administrator when finished.
B. Use strong passwords.
C. Turn off the computer when finished.
D. Disable the save password function on web pages.
E. Make sure to clean the keyboard when finished.
F. Make sure to log out of websites when done.

QUESTION 44
When operating under optimal network conditions, which of the following has the HIGHEST reliability?

A. Bluetooth
B. Wired
C. Cellular
D. WiFi

QUESTION 45
A user needs to download tax documents from a financial website. Which of the following is the website MOST likely to use for transmission of the tax document to the user's browser?

A. HTTP
B. HTTPS
C. SFTP

D. FTP

QUESTION 46
Which of the following are secure network protocols? (Select TWO).

A. IMAP
B. FTPS
C. SMTP
D. HTTPS
E. DNS

QUESTION 47
Which of the following will allow the easiest and fastest way to share a single file between two modern smartphones without joining the same WiFi network?

A. Micro SD card
B. Bluetooth
C. USB connection
D. Infrared

QUESTION 48
Which of the following BEST describes the pros and cons of a home wired network?

A. Low throughput, low mobility, high availability, high latency, high security
B. High throughput, high mobility, low availability, low latency, high security
C. High throughput, low mobility, high availability, low latency, high security
D. Low throughput, high mobility, low availability, high latency, lowsecurity

QUESTION 49
A technician has just finished setting up a SOHO wireless router but the client does not want the PC on the wireless network for security reasons. The technician connects an RJ-45 cable to the computer and the router, but does not receive network connectivity. Which of the following is the NEXT step to diagnose the problem?

A. Change the IP address on the computer to match the router.
B. Reseat the power cable on the computer and reboot.
C. Check for link light activity on the computer and the router.
D. Change the hostname of the router to match the computer's network.

QUESTION 50
Which of the following is an advantage of using cloud-based collaborative applications and storage, rather than local applications and storage?

A. Decreased software licensing costs
B. Higher security encryption
C. Limited storage space for files
D. Increased accessibility to files

QUESTION 51
Which of the following data connections would provide a user the BEST Internet availability while traveling?

A. Workstation with only RJ-45 connectors
B. Smartphone with cellular service
C. Laptop with Bluetooth wireless connectivity
D. Tablet connected to a SOHO wireless network

QUESTION 52
A technician is configuring a wireless router for a small office and the business owner would like the wireless network to be secured using the strongest encryption possible. Which of the following should the technician choose?

A. WPA2
B. WAP
C. WPA
D. WEP

QUESTION 53
A user's laptop hard drive contains sensitive information. The user often plugs the laptop into the corporate network. A sensitive file from the laptop has been found on another user's laptop. How could the user have prevented this breach?

A. Disable file and print sharing on the laptop.
B. Delete unused drives from network.
C. Remove shared keys from the key ring.
D. Set the read-only attribute on the files.

QUESTION 54
Joe, a user, needs to store a large amount of data, but does not have enough space on his local computer. Which of the following are the BEST options for him to use? (Select TWO).

A. Network attached storage
B. External hard drive

C. Optical drive
D. USB thumb drive
E. Another computer

QUESTION 55
When connecting a printer to a network, which of the following is needed to complete the process? (Select TWO).

A. IP address
B. User's password
C. Computer's name
D. Subnet mask
E. HTTP port
F. Fax number

QUESTION 56
A technician is setting up a computer that was shipped. After everything is plugged in, the computer will not turn on. Which of the following should the technician do FIRST to identify the issue?

A. Check for physical damage on the computer.
B. Search for a solution on the Internet.
C. Reference the manufacturer's documentation.
D. Ensure the power supply is set at the correct voltage.

QUESTION 57
Ann, a user, wishes to free space in her documents folder. Which of the following is the BEST characteristic to sort by in order to ensure that the most space is freed by deleting the least amount of files?

A. Date modified
B. File path
C. Size
D. Extension

QUESTION 58
Where can a user find the latest updates, upgrades, or firmware for an electronic device that the vendor supports?

A. Internet search engine
B. Internet forum
C. Technical community groups

D. OEM website

QUESTION 59
When applying ergonomics to a workstation area, which of the following are the MOST important to consider? (Select TWO).

A. Proper sitting position
B. Amount of time computer will be used
C. Clarity of the display
D. Proper keyboard and mouse height
E. Number of speakers in sound system
F. Brightness and contrast of the display

QUESTION 60
An RoHS label on hardware indicates which of the following?

A. The hardware produces EMI when used.
B. The hardware is certified to be energy efficient.
C. The hardware provides battery backup for power outages.
D. The hardware needs to be properly disposed.

QUESTION 61
Ann, a user, reports that her computer was working this morning, but now the screen is blank. The power indicator for the monitor is on. Pressing the space bar or mouse does not fix the problem. Which of the following is the cause?

A. The monitor power cable is unplugged.
B. The video cable has become disconnected.
C. The video driver is not installed.
D. The operating system has encountered a stop error.
E. The screen saver has activated.

QUESTION 62
Which of the following will allow a user to move a file from one folder to another using the LEAST number of steps, while ensuring that the file is removed from its original location?

A. Open the file from its original location, save it to the new location, and delete it from the original location.
B. Cut the file from its original location and paste it to the new location.
C. Rename the file in its original location to a name that is not already taken in the new location.
D. Copy the file from its original location and paste it to the new location.

QUESTION 63
Which of the following permissions is required to run a .bat file?

A. Delete
B. Execute
C. Write
D. Modify

QUESTION 64
After initial OS and application installation on a laptop, an application warns that it will only work 24 more times. Which of the following should be done NEXT?

A. The application has to be registered to the user.
B. The application must be upgraded to a 64-bit version.
C. The application must be activated.
D. The application needs to be reinstalled.

QUESTION 65
An employee's new computer came with a free 30-day trial version of antivirus software. The employee's company provides enterprise antivirus software from a different vendor. Which of the following should the employee do in order to use a full version of antivirus software?

A. Enter the company product key for the antivirus software, enabling the full version.
B. Uninstall the current version antivirus software and install the companyversion.
C. Verify Internet connectivity and run online virus scanningsoftware.
D. Update the trial antivirus software to the latest version.

QUESTION 66
A user has finished setting up a new computer. Now the operating system requires activation, but the user discovers the computer has no Internet connection. Which of the following should the user do FIRST?

A. Contact technical support.
B. Reboot the computer.
C. Check the Ethernet cable.
D. Review manufacturer's website.

QUESTION 67
Which of the following is a feature of a basic power strip?

A. Protects against lightning strikes
B. Provides multiple outlets for power
C. Generates power for devices
D. Provides battery backup for devices

QUESTION 68
Which of the following should be performed after a backup has been completed?

A. Delete the backup
B. Verify the backup
C. Save the backup
D. Schedule the backup

QUESTION 69
Which of the following is a file on a computer that links to another program or file somewhere else on the same computer?

A. Shortcut
B. URL
C. Attachment
D. FTP

QUESTION 70
Which of the following defines why backup verification is important?

A. To ensure that the backup runs as quickly as possible
B. To ensure that the backup can be stored indefinitely
C. To ensure that the backup can be saved to the cloud
D. To ensure that the backup contains usable data

QUESTION 71
A home computer that has been in operation for more than five years is now suffering from random shutdowns during the day. The PC is set up in an enclosed cubby built into the home office desk. Which of the following is MOST likely plaguing the PC?

A. The PC was switched over to 240v operation mode
B. Dust accumulation
C. The PC's BIOS is severely out-of-date, causing PSU issues
D. EMI

QUESTION 72

A user installed a new scanner on a desktop personal computer without any documentation. The scanner powers on, the lamp turns on, and then the unit stops with a failure light lit. Which of the following should the user do FIRST?

A. Go to the scanner manufacturer's website and download the current installation information.
B. Check the personal computer manufacturer's support website for information about scanner installation.
C. Find a scanner user group website and ask for help.
D. Update the scanner firmware and drivers, then reinstall the scanner.

QUESTION 73
Which of the following can a user configure on an operating system so that an audible sound is made when an error message is displayed?

A. Encryption
B. Hot keys
C. Accessibility options
D. Screen captures

QUESTION 74
Which of the following should be done to reduce physical safety hazards around a newly installed computer?

A. Verify all connections are seated properly.
B. Avoid placing other computers nearby.
C. Bundle loose cables with zip ties or Velcro straps.
D. Attach all peripherals to the computer.

QUESTION 75
A user with an outdated operating system is consistently browsing sensitive websites such as banking, email, and corporate intranets. The Internet browser of choice is one that has already lost patch support and is not updated anymore. Which of the following actions will remedy this situation?

A. Uninstall all unused browser extensions and toolbars to help reduce risks.
B. Convert the user's account to an admin level account, to provide better overall security.
C. Move to an alternate browser that still has consistent security update support.
D. Install multiple anti-malware and firewall products to harden the computing experience.

QUESTION 76

Which of the following connectors is MOST often used to connect a computer to a network?

A. RJ-45
B. RJ-11
C. IDE
D. eSATA

QUESTION 77
A user is installing a new scanner on a computer. Which of the following MOST likely needs to be installed in order for this equipment to work?

A. License key
B. OS update
C. Firmware
D. Driver

QUESTION 78
Which of the following software is used to reduce the size of a file or folder?

A. Desktop publishing
B. Basic database
C. Compression
D. Anti-malware

QUESTION 79
Which of the following is used with a touch screen to increase accuracy?

A. Touchpad
B. Stylus pen
C. Joystick
D. Trackball

QUESTION 80
Which of the following internal components is used for temporary data storage in a workstation?

A. Power supply
B. CPU
C. RAM
D. Hard drive

QUESTION 81
Which of the following is used for temporary storage of program data that is cleared when the computer is turned off?

A. CPU
B. SSD
C. Hard drive
D. System memory

QUESTION 82
Which of the following connectors supports both high definition video and audio?

A. S-video
B. Component
C. HDMI
D. DVI

QUESTION 83
Which of the following BEST describes malicious software that demands the end-user pay a fee or face the destruction of their files?

A. Trojan
B. Virus
C. Spyware
D. Ransomware

QUESTION 84
Which of the following should be done to reduce the risk of having sensitive passwords compromised while browsing the Internet?

A. Enable software firewalls to block unknown ports
B. Disable autofill of forms and passwords
C. Enable screensavers and time-outs on the computer
D. Use ad-blocking software on the computer

QUESTION 85
Which of the following would be the MOST efficient way to transport a file from one location on a local hard drive to a different location on the same hard drive?

A. Rename
B. Cut

C. Move
D. Save

QUESTION 86
A student wishes to share contacts with another student's mobile device. Which of the following would be the easiest method to use?

A. Network attached storage
B. Bluetooth sharing
C. Local hard drive
D. Peer-to-Peer network

QUESTION 87
When setting up a new desktop, which of the following should be performed FIRST?

A. Configure user accounts
B. Plug in cables
C. Install security software
D. Configure wireless network settings

QUESTION 88
A user, Joe, wants to install an application on his computer. Which of the following factors should he be aware of before beginning?

A. The computer has the proper hard drive drivers installed.
B. The computer is connected to a secure wireless network.
C. Check for any updates for the application.
D. The computer meets the application's minimum requirements.

QUESTION 89
Which of the following applications would a user employ to write a business letter?

A. Spreadsheet software
B. Word processor
C. Desktop publishing
D. Presentation software

QUESTION 90
Which of the following devices transmits and receives printed images over a telephone line?

A. Monitor
B. Fax
C. Scanner
D. Webcam

QUESTION 91
Which of the following is considered an open-source operating system?

A. Windows
B. Chrome OS
C. Mac OS X
D. Linux

QUESTION 92
A technician wants to keep a router up to date. Which of the following MUST be updated regularly?

A. SSID
B. Administrator password
C. Wireless encryption
D. Firmware

QUESTION 93
The extension .rtf is an example of which of the following file types?

A. Document
B. Executable
C. Audio
D. Speadsheet

QUESTION 94
Which of the following are examples of video connectors? (Select TWO).

A. VGA
B. Serial
C. HDMI
D. eSATA
E. PS/2

QUESTION 95
When setting up a new computer, where does a user change the date and time?

A. Peripheral configuration
B. Localization settings
C. Screen resolution
D. eSATA settings

QUESTION 96
A user wants to have the latest security patches and bug fixes installed on a computer. Which of the following is the BEST method to achieve this?

A. Configure anti-malware updates
B. Manually update before each use
C. Update every six months
D. Schedule automatic updates

QUESTION 97
A user is accessing an online bank account for the first time via an Internet browser. Which of the following should the user check? (Select TWO).

A. HTTPS before the URL
B. Exclamation point on the status bar
C. Lock symbol in the address bar
D. HTTP before the URL
E. Skull/crossbones symbol in the corner

QUESTION 98
Which of the following CPU cooling types is BEST in a dusty environment?

A. Liquid cooling
B. Open case
C. Case fan
D. Heat sink fan

QUESTION 99
To reduce the risk of installing unapproved or possibly malicious apps on a smartphone, a user should:

A. Download apps from a user-supported community.
B. Use a search engine to identify safe apps.
C. Update the firmware to the latest version.
D. Utilize the vendor-provided app store.

QUESTION 100
Which of the following computer connector types was designed specifically for allowing high-speed external hard drive transfers?

A. DVI
B. USB
C. eSATA
D. HDMI

QUESTION 101
Which of the following is a common way to prevent physical theft of a laptop or workstation?

A. Shred any sensitive information to prior to disposal.
B. Avoid storing passwords near the computer.
C. Practice good awareness skills when entering passwords/PINs.
D. Cable and lock device securely attached to a solid object.

QUESTION 102
Ann, a user, is browsing shopping websites on the Internet when she receives a pop-up message on her screen indicating a virus has been detected by the antivirus software. Which of the following actions should be performed NEXT?

A. Ignore the message because it is likely adware.
B. Run a scan on the entire local drive.
C. Clear temporary files and folders.
D. Minimize the alert and continue browsing the Internet.

QUESTION 103
A technician needs to troubleshoot a user's computer. The user leaves personal credentials written on a piece of paper for the technician. Which of the following principles has the user violated?

A. Password confidentiality
B. Password complexity
C. Password reuse
D. Password expiration

QUESTION 104
Joe, a user, has many applications on his computer and is trying to use software management best practices. Which of the following should he consider?

A. Install a desktop cleanup application.
B. Uninstall unneeded applications.
C. Load each application one at a time.
D. Manage the use of internal memory.

QUESTION 105
A user's government identification number, birth date, and current address are considered which of the following?

A. IMAP
B. HTTP
C. PII
D. HTTPS

QUESTION 106
A user, Ann, calls the manufacturer of a software product she purchased, but is denied assistance because the product is no longer supported. Which of the following options is a BEST next choice?

A. P2P software sharing service
B. Original instruction manual
C. Online user forum
D. PC manufacturer's website

QUESTION 107
Which of the following software types BEST facilitates collaboration?

A. Personal information manager
B. Video editing software
C. Instant messaging software
D. CAD software

QUESTION 108
To increase security, which of the following is the BEST feature to disable on a mobile device when not in use?

A. Wireless
B. GPS
C. Network
D. NFC

QUESTION 109
Which of the following data connectivity options is the BEST to use when both high availability and reliability are required?

A. WiFi
B. Bluetooth
C. Cellular
D. Wired

QUESTION 110
A technician has added an external hard drive to a personal computer. The hard drive is powered on, but the computer does not see the new hard disk. Which of the following is the FIRST thing the technician should check?

A. The power cable
B. The OS version for compatibility
C. The hard drive firmware revision
D. The data cable

QUESTION 111
Which of the following is the MOST secure password?

A. Have-A-Nice-Day
B. HAVE-A-NICE-DAY
C. have-a-nice-day12
D. hav3-@-Nic3-D@Y14

QUESTION 112
Which of the following is the primary goal in performing a backup verification?

A. Ensure backup data can be correctly restored
B. Prove the media has sufficient space for the data
C. Configure frequency of backups
D. Adhere to legal backup storage requirements

QUESTION 113
Which of the following file types is used to consolidate a group of files?

A. .rtf
B. .m3u
C. .avi
D. .rar

QUESTION 114
Which of the following keys should be pressed to enable access to various menus?

A. ALT
B. SHIFT
C. TAB
D. CTRL

QUESTION 115
Ann, a user, has an external monitor that will not turn on. Her laptop has activity lights and is plugged into the same power strip. Which of the following should be checked FIRST to begin troubleshooting this issue?

A. The power strip
B. The monitor video cable
C. The laptop power cable
D. The monitor power cable

QUESTION 116
Which of the following methods are MOST likely used to reduce the internal temperature of a computer?

A. Install a protective cover
B. Reduce display brightness
C. Air circulation
D. Electronic recycling
E. Liquid cooling

QUESTION 117
A technician is setting up a router and would like to increase the security level. Which of the following actions will achieve this?

A. Installing anti-malware on the router
B. Changing the default admin password
C. Increasing transmission power
D. Configuring multifactor logon authentication

QUESTION 118
Which of the following data connections can span the FARTHEST distance?

A. WiFi

B. Dial-up
C. Satellite
D. Cable

QUESTION 119
Which of the following functions can transfer a file between folders and deletes it from the original folder?

A. Edit
B. Move
C. Copy
D. Paste

QUESTION 120
An end-user has 16GB of RAM installed on a computer system. Which of the following describes why the OS only uses a maximum of 4GB of RAM?

A. The operating system is 16-bit.
B. The computer has corrupted RAM.
C. The computer has a defective motherboard.
D. The operating system is 32-bit.
E. The computer has a virus.

QUESTION 121
A technician just installed a new computer. Which of the following is the BEST way to manage the cables?

A. Line the cables up neatly and wrap them together with cable ties.
B. Leave the cables loose to prevent interference between wires.
C. Nail the cables to the wall.
D. Tuck the cables neatly underneath the carpet.

QUESTION 122
A printer is migrated between offices. All the wires are connected properly, but the new workstation cannot find the printer. Which of the following should the technician install?

A. OS
B. Updates
C. Drivers
D. Application

QUESTION 123
A user wants to run a major update on a laptop. Which of the following should be considered before running any major updates?

A. Restore folders from back up
B. Change administrator account password
C. Back up important folders
D. Print all personal documents

QUESTION 124
Which of the following adds a basic security measure to a wireless device?

A. Hands-free headset
B. Screen lock feature
C. Airplane mode
D. Clip-on case

QUESTION 125
Which of the following system utilities allows a user to configure multiple monitors in the OS?

A. Color management
B. Device manager
C. GPU driver
D. Display

QUESTION 126
Joe, a user, reports that his neck and back are hurting after being at his desk for the whole day. Which of the following are the possible causes of the problem? (Select TWO).

A. The keyboard is not ergonomic.
B. The monitor does not have a screen protector.
C. The monitor height is not adjusted to Joe's needs.
D. Joe is not using a wrist rest with the keyboard.
E. The chair is not properly adjusted to Joe's needs.

QUESTION 127
Which of the following are core peripherals needed to use a desktop PC? (Select THREE).

A. Monitor
B. Keyboard

C. Printer
D. Mouse
E. Speakers
F. Mouse pad
G. Webcam

QUESTION 128
A user purchases a new desktop computer and requires assistance setting it up. Which of the following describes the BEST resource the user should reference?

A. Technical community group
B. Local retail store technical support
C. Internet search engine
D. Manufacturer documentation

QUESTION 129
Which of the following is used for telepresence?

A. VoIP telephone
B. Webcam
C. Remote desktop
D. Touchscreen

QUESTION 130
Which of the following storage media provides the FASTEST speeds when backing up large data files?

A. Offsite storage
B. Network attached storage
C. Locally attached storage
D. Cloud-based storage

QUESTION 131
Which of the following security threats is classified as license theft?

A. Entering the neighbor's software key
B. Using software to reveal a password
C. Searching through the trash for passwords
D. Watching what a user types on screen

QUESTION 132

The manufacturer of a SOHO router has released a security fix for the router. Which of the following methods should be used to apply the fix?

A. Change the admin password.
B. Apply new WEP key.
C. Update the firmware.
D. Hold the reset button.

QUESTION 133
Joe, a user, wants to back up all the data on his home computers to a safe medium that will survive a house fire. Which of the following if the BEST choice?

A. Blu-ray disc
B. Cloud-based
C. USB HDD
D. FireWire HDD

QUESTION 134
Which of the following allows users to print to another user's local printer?

A. Network printing
B. Bluetooth printing
C. Print sharing
D. Peer-to-peer sharing

QUESTION 135
Which of the following allows for an audio and video signal to be sent via a single cable?

A. HDMI
B. VGA
C. RGB
D. SATA

QUESTION 136
Which of the following is used by an email account to receive email?

A. DNS
B. SMTP
C. SFTP
D. SNMP
E. POP3

QUESTION 137
Which of the following is true about a user wanting to run a 64-bit software program on a 32-bit OS?

A. The program cannot run natively on a 32-bit OS.
B. The program will run with reduced functionality.
C. The program can only run in compatibility mode.
D. The program can run only if the computer hardware supports 64-bit.

QUESTION 138
To ensure that a user is hardening computer resources properly, the user should do which of the following? (Select two.)

A. Use one account for all family members.
B. Look for open wireless network.
C. Recognize suspicious hyperlinks.
D. Install and update threat prevention software.
E. Use a password-protected screen saver.
F. Disable system timeouts.

QUESTION 139
Which of the following are examples of mobile OSs for cellular services? (Select two.)

A. iOS
B. Mac OS X
C. Chrome OS
D. Android
E. Windows XP

QUESTION 140
Which of the following is a type of printing technology commonly used today?

A. Infrared
B. eSATA
C. Laser
D. Flatbed

QUESTION 141
Which of the following connection methods requires line-of-sight to be effective?

A. Fiber optics

B. Infrared
C. Cellular
D. Wi-Fi

QUESTION 142
A technician wants to test a new OS version locally without interfering with a production installation. Which of the following is the BEST technology to use?

A. Cloud application software
B. Virtualization software
C. Telepresence software
D. Collaboration software

QUESTION 143
Which of the following are MOST likely to be configured during the initial setup of an OS on a basic workstation? (Select two.)

A. Antivirus settings
B. License keys
C. Email setup
D. Localization settings
E. Printer configuration

QUESTION 144
When logging in to a laptop, which of the following is an example of multifactor authentication?

A. Logging on via key fob, password, and fingerprint reader
B. Entering an account number, PIN, and password to log in
C. A technician using the fingerprint reader and a retina scan
D. A user entering a strong password to log in

QUESTION 145
An employee who is working for a small business would like to prevent shoulder surfing. Which of the following should the employee do?

A. Lock the computer.
B. Purchase a privacy screen.
C. Enable encryption.
D. Create a strong password.

QUESTION 146
A user is attempting to open a file and receives a pop-up message stating that the action cannot be accomplished. This is MOST likely a result of which of the following?

A. The user is not logged into the system properly.
B. The file is a read-only file.
C. The user is not granted permission to access the file.
D. The file attribute is set to hidden.

QUESTION 147
Which of the following are basic functions to use when working only with files and folders in an OS? (Select two.)

A. Maximize
B. Run
C. Copy
D. Exit
E. Minimize
F. Rename

QUESTION 148
Which of the following would a user need in order to connect to a public wireless hotspot at a local coffee shop?

A. SSID
B. User name
C. IP address
D. Wireless channel

QUESTION 149
Ann, a user, is using a mobile device at a local coffee shop where she connects to an open Wi-Fi hotspot. Which of the following is a risk that should be considered while using the hotspot?

A. Data is not encrypted.
B. Browser history is searchable.
C. Passwords are secure.
D. Firewall use is not necessary.

QUESTION 150
Which of the following describes sleep mode for a computer?

A. No energy usage with session data stored in RAM
B. Low energy usage with session data stored in RAM
C. Low energy usage with session data stored on the HDD\SSD
D. No energy usage with session data stored on the HDD\SSD

QUESTION 151
A user wants to securely back up data for recovery in case of a natural disaster. Which of the following is the BEST solution? (Select two.)

A. Back up to a NAS on-site.
B. Back up to tape and send off-site.
C. Use cloud-based backup.
D. Encrypt all backup copies.
E. Keep backup copies on multiple hard drives.

QUESTION 152
A technician needs to connect a user's computer to the network. Which of the following device types would the technician install?

A. Modem
B. Ethernet card
C. Graphics card
D. Daughterboard

QUESTION 153
Ann and Joe, both users, share the same computer. They both log on using the same account. Ann is concerned that Joe may review her Internet activity. Which of the following can be implemented to prevent both users from reviewing each other's Internet activity?

A. Encrypt the computer's hard drive.
B. Each user should use a different browsertype.
C. Use a password to protect the shared account.
D. Configure the browser to clear history upon exit.

QUESTION 154
Which of the following are the FASTEST ways to send a copy of a physical document to a remote user? (Select two.)

A. Scan and email a copy of the document.
B. Use document transcription software.
C. Retype the document on the user's computer.

D. Fax a copy of the document to the user.
E. Copy and mail the document to the user.

QUESTION 155
Which of the following devices may be required for video conferencing? (Select three.)

A. Speakers
B. Touch screen
C. Microphone
D. Webcam
E. DVD drive
F. Projector

QUESTION 156
Which of the following requires user interaction in order to spread?

A. Worm
B. Adware
C. Ransomware
D. Virus

QUESTION 157
Which of the following are good practices to follow when creating a password? (Select two.)

A. Use personal identifiable information.
B. Use the same password on multiple systems.
C. Use a phrase that is easy to remember.
D. Use mixed case letters.
E. Use special characters.

QUESTION 158
Joe, a user, has installed a new SOHO wireless router. The router keeps dropping PC connections. Which of the following should be check?

A. SSID
B. MAC address
C. Firmware
D. Password

QUESTION 159

A traveling business user is utilizing an LTE cellular connection that provides good coverage but experiences numerous outages during a given week. This would be classified as which of the following?

A. High mobility and low reliability
B. High mobility and high latency
C. High availability and low mobility
D. High availability and low throughput

Answers Exam 1

Question 1: D Question 2: D Question 3: A Question 4: B Question 5: D Question 6: C Question 7: A Question 8: C Question 9: A Question 10: A Question 11: B Question 12: C Question 13: A Question 14: C Question 15: C Question 16: A Question 17: A Question 18: C Question 19: D Question 20: B Question 21: BD Question 22: B Question 23: D Question 24: A Question 25: AB Question 26: D Question 27: D Question 28: A Question 29: BD Question 30: D	Question 31: B Question 32: D Question 33: B

Answers Exam 2

Question 1: D	Question 31: C	Question 61: B
Question 2: B	Question 32: A	Question 62: B
Question 3: D	Question 33: A	Question 63: B
Question 4: B	Question 34: B	Question 64: C
Question 5: A	Question 35: A	Question 65: B
Question 6: C	Question 36: D	Question 66: C
Question 7: D	Question 37: C	Question 67: B
Question 8: B	Question 38: C	Question 68: B
Question 9: A	Question 39: ACE	Question 69: A
Question 10: E	Question 40: B	Question 70: D
Question 11: B	Question 41: B	Question 71: B
Question 12: DEFH	Question 42: B	Question 72: A
Question 13: A	Question 43: DF	Question 73: C
Question 14: B	Question 44: B	Question 74: C
Question 15: C	Question 45: B	Question 75: C
Question 16: BC	Question 46: BD	Question 76: A
Question 17: D	Question 47: B	Question 77: D
Question 18: B	Question 48: C	Question 78: C
Question 19: D	Question 49: C	Question 79: B
Question 20: A	Question 50: D	Question 80: C
Question 21: B	Question 51: B	Question 81: D
Question 22: AE	Question 52: A	Question 82: C
Question 23: B	Question 53: A	Question 83: D
Question 24: C	Question 54: AB	Question 84: B
Question 25: E	Question 55: AD	Question 85: C
Question 26: C	Question 56: D	Question 86: B
Question 27: C	Question 57: C	Question 87: B
Question 28: DE	Question 58: D	Question 88: D
Question 29: CD	Question 59: AD	Question 89: B
Question 30: B	Question 60: D	Question 90: B

Question 91: D	Question 121: A	Question 151: CD
Question 92: D	Question 122: C	Question 152: B
Question 93: A	Question 123: C	Question 153: D
Question 94: AC	Question 124: B	Question 154: AD
Question 95: B	Question 125: D	Question 155: ACD
Question 96: D	Question 126: CE	Question 156: C
Question 97: AC	Question 127: ABD	Question 157: DE
Question 98: A	Question 128: D	Question 158: C
Question 99: D	Question 129: B	Question 159: A
Question 100: C	Question 130: C	
Question 101: D	Question 131: A	
Question 102: B	Question 132: C	
Question 103: A	Question 133: B	
Question 104: B	Question 134: C	
Question 105: C	Question 135: A	
Question 106: C	Question 136: E	
Question 107: C	Question 137: A	
Question 108: D	Question 138: DE	
Question 109: D	Question 139: AD	
Question 110: D	Question 140: C	
Question 111: D	Question 141: B	
Question 112: A	Question 142: B	
Question 113: D	Question 143: BD	
Question 114: A	Question 144: A	
Question 115: D	Question 145: B	
Question 116: CE	Question 146: C	
Question 117: B	Question 147: CF	
Question 118: C	Question 148: A	
Question 119: B	Question 149: A	
Question 120: D	Question 150: B	

Good Luck

in your Exam

Made in the USA
Middletown, DE
12 February 2021